MW00908005

ITALIAN FOR BEGINNERS

A Practical Guide To Learn The Basics of Italian in 10 Days

MANUEL DE CORTES

TABLE OF CONTENTS

INTRODUCTION

Dear reader,
I firstly want to express my thanks to you for buying and downloading the book *"Italian for Beginners: A practical guide to learn the basics of Italian language"*.

I also want to tell you that you're awesome for wanting to learn this beautiful and extraordinary language.

This book contains proven steps and strategies on how to learn the basics of the Italian language. The main purpose of this book is to help you master the basics of two-way communication using the Italian language. As you go through the pages of this book, do not be discouraged if you cannot pronounce everything perfectly immediately. Learning a new language will take time and this book will be your companion through this adventure.

Consider this book as the first BIG step you are taking in order to become fluent in Italian. It provides you with a foundation on which you can build on as you learn and master the Italian language.

Thanks again for purchasing this book,
I hope you enjoy it!
Manuel De Cortes

CHAPTER 1:
ESSENTIAL ITALIAN BASICS

It's fascinating that so many people travel the world seeing different countries, tasting the cuisine and soaking up the culture yet they fail to learn a few basic words such as *please* and *thank you*. Within the pages of this book, you will learn the basics of the Italian language. Throughout the course of this book, remember one thing: keep a steady pace and don't try to bite of more than you can chew. It is better for you to master 10 words than to tackle 50 ones that you can't recall by heart.

Italians are more responsive to foreigners that learn (and make an effort) to speak their language even if not pronounced perfectly. To them, this is a sign of respect towards them and their culture. Basic knowledge of the language – common phrases, terms and expressions – will help you feel more acquainted with the Italian customs and may even prevent unwanted [and avoidable] complications.
As you read through this book, it is highly recommended that you carry with you a recorder. As you course through the conversations and dialogues in this book, you can record yourself as you pronounce words. That way, you will be able to review your progress and listen to the way you enunciate each word and – syllable.

Some chapters contain a list of common key words and phrases that are used in everyday Italian conversations. Go through these words on a regular basis to help you memorize the words by heart. Learning a new language takes a lot of memory work. And in order to get something into your system, repetition is the key.

Articulation guide:

The Italian language is often [if not always] *pronounced as it is spelled.* There are certain rules that you must follow when it comes to pronouncing vowels and consonants. It is suggested that you read this guide before tackling words and phrases. The first column contains the vowel or consonant; the second column refers to an English word that serves as a guideline during articulation while the last column are examples of Italian words.

Note that some letters have more than one form of pronunciation. Pronunciation may change depending on the combination of letters.

Vowels	English word (To pronounce like)	Italian word
a	Math	Casa
e	Tell	Venti
	Hey	Penna
i	Pizza	Lira
o	Pot	Opera
	Port	Totale
u	Mule	Turista
Consonants	**English word**	**Italian word**
c 2 sounds: Before *e* or *i*: /ch/ Before *h, a, o* and *u*: /k/	Chocolate Chemistry	*Ciao* *Scusi*
g 2 sounds: Before *e* or *i*: /j/ Before *h, a, o* and *u*: /g/	Geography Grass	*Gentile* *Spaghetti*

h	Always silent. Refer to consonants *c* and *g* for guidelines.		
r	Pronounced as is but should roll naturally from the tongue.		
s 2 sounds: "s" "se"	Simple Hose	*Sì* *Musica*	
z 2 sounds: "ts" "tz"	Hats Tzar	*Grazie* *Zero*	

Special considerations:

- Rules on pronouncing words with double consonants: Words with containing double consonants are pronounced in a similar manner except that the sound drags along for a longer period of time. There is a split second delay when saying these words whereas single consonants are pronounced continuously or fluidly.
  - **Caro - Ca<u>rr</u>o**
  - **Dona - Do<u>nn</u>a**
  - **Pala - Pa<u>ll</u>a**
- Combining letters
  There are certain rules you must observe when pronouncing letters that are combined together:
  - **ch :** /k/ - like <u>*chi*</u>*aroscuro*
  - **gh :** /g/ - like *spa<u>gh</u>etti*
  - **gli :** /lli/ - like *gi<u>gli</u>*
  - **gn :** /ñ/ - like *sauvi<u>gn</u>on*
  - **qu :** /kwa/ - like <u>*qu*</u>*arto*
  - **sc** – has 2 sounds
    - Followed by **e** or **i:** /sh/ - like <u>*sc*</u>*ialle*
    - Followed by **h, a, o** or **u:** /sk/ - like <u>*sc*</u>*olaro*

- Emphasis on syllables
  Similar to the English language, stress or emphasis on particular syllables is required in order to deliver the right meaning of a particular word. Unfortunately, there is no universal rule in *Italiano* when it comes to giving stress to a syllable of a word. This is something that you need to memorize on your own. Note that throughout this book, you will notice letters with stress symbols on the top a syllable. This serves as your guide when pronouncing words.

Tips on articulation:
You may find it quite hard to pronounce certain words at first. It can get frustrating, but you must remember to relax when you are pronouncing words. The tenser you get, the less likely you'll be able to say things properly. If a word is too "big" or complicated to pronounce, dissect it into syllables, and then determine where the emphasis should be. Enunciate slowly and then gradually gain more speed.

Keep in mind that repetition is your friend in these circumstances. Our end goal here is to be able to communicate with other so this means that you must deliver each word as clearly as possible. If you're having a hard time on pronouncing words, go over the points below:
- Listen or go over native speakers. There is a lot of audio and video material available online that is at your disposal. By listening to native speakers, you will be able to get the proper pronunciation and emphasis on particular words.
- Have a recorder on hand. When you are practicing your articulation, try to record yourself. Hearing yourself while you speak can be different from reviewing your articulation over a voice recorder. The latter provides you with a different insight into how you communicate to a third party. Also, this helps you to compare your skills with that of a native speaker.

- If you happen to have a friend that is fluent in Italian, you can ask them to help you go over your recordings. Asking someone who is fluent in the language can give you a good constructive criticism on which points you should improve on. While you're at it, ask them to list down words that you might have mispronounced so you can focus on these.

Now that we've tackled the basics of articulation, let's have a short vocabulary lesson. Below are a few common Italian phrases. Try to pronounce each word out loud and see how it rolls on your tongue.

Buongiorno [bwon-jorno]	Good morning Good day Good afternoon
Buonasera [bwona-sayra]	Good evening Good afternoon
Buonanotte [bwona not-tay]	Good night
Arrivederci [ar-ree-vay-dayr-chee]	Goodbye See you soon
Arrivederla [ah-ree-veh-deh-rr-la]	Goodbye So long See you soon
Ciao [chou]	Hello Hi So long
Signore [see-nuor-ray]	Sir Gentleman Lord
Signor [see-nuor]	Mister Mr.
Uomo ['womo]	Man Mankind

Signora [see-nuor-ra]	*Ma'am* *Madam* *Miss* *Ms.* *Missis* *Mrs.* *Lady*
Donna [don-na]	*Woman*
Signorina [see-nuor-ree-na]	*Young lady* *Miss* *Young woman*
Sì [see]	*Of course* *Yes*
No	*No*
Per favore [per fav-o-ray]	*Please*
Grazie [grats-yay]	*Thanks* *Thank you*
Prego [pray-go]	*You're welcome* *Don't mention it!*
Prego? [pray-gó]	*Pardon?* ** (Used when you wish to have something repeated)
Scusi [scoos-ee]	*Excuse me* *I am sorry* **(Can also be used in order to call someone's attention)
Mi dispiace [me dis-pee-arch-ay]	*I beg your pardon* *I am [very] sorry*
Come sta? [komay sta]	*How are you?* *How are you doing?*
Bene, grazie [bay-nay, grat-see]	*Well, thank you!*

E Lei? [ay lay]	*And you?* *And how about you?*
Molto bene, grazie [molto bay-nay grats-yay]	*Very well, thank you!*
Non troppo bene [non tropeu bay-nay]	*Not too well...*
Non ćè male [non ke meil] **(ćè = the combination of letters is pronounced as "che")*	*Not too bad / Not that bad...*
Parlare [par'lare]	*To speak* *To talk (a lot)* *To chatter*
Parla inglese/italiano? [par-la]	*Do you speak English* *Do you speak Italian?*
Parli più lentamente [par-li piu len-ta-mente]	*To speak more gradually* *To speak slowly*
Va bene [va bay-nay]	*Okay* *That's okay* *Alright* *Certainly*

Now that you know a few common phrases, try to repeat them about 15-20 times over. If you are recording yourself, try to review how you pronounce and which syllables you put stress on. Be cautious of how you deliver your words.

Practice conversations and dialogues (Dialoghi)

Below are three conversations to help you practice rudimentary Italian conversation. Play both parts and try to visualize having a conversation with a native speaker. If you wish to make the scenario more realistic, have a native speaker help you practice these dialogues.

- Dialogue 1: Common greeting.
  Signor Francesco: *Buongiorno, signora Moretti!*
  Signora Moretti: *Buongiorno, signor Francesco. Come sta?*
  Signor Francesco: *Molto bene, grazie. E lei?*
  Signora Moretti: *Bene. Arrivederci signor!*
  Signor Francesco: *Arrivederci.*
- Dialogue 2: Asking if a person speaks English
  Mr. Smith: *Buongiorno, signore! Parla inglese?*
  Signor Malta: *Buongiorno, signore! Sì, molto bene.*

Quick tips on syntax and proper use of words:
- When greeting someone...
  - **Buongiorno** – is used until 4 in the afternoon during the summer season; just before dark during the winter.
  - **Buonasera** – used after *Buongiorno* when it is already dark.
  - **Buonanotte** – used when one is going to bed or when it is time to call it a night.
- When bidding someone goodbye...
  - **Arrivederci** – used when saying goodbye to someone you plan to see again soon; used also when leaving a place of business.
  - **Arrivederla** – a more formal expression. Used when talking to someone of a high position or in a professional situation.
  - **Ciao** – has a double meaning of *hello* and *goodbye;* only used in an informal or casual setting; never in a formal or professional scenario.
- Appropriate titles: addressing yourself and others
  - **Signor** is the direct equivalent of *Mister/ Mr.* in the English language hence it should always be followed by a surname.
  - **Signore** is used when the name of the person you are speaking to is unknown.

The same applies for women with the use of **Signora; signorina.** Note that the former is used to address older or adult women whereas the latter is used to address unmarried and young women.

- How to properly and politely ask a question
  Similar to the English language, when asking a question you must place the proper intonation at the end of your sentence or phrase to indicate that you are making a query. The same goes with writing.

Practice situations:
See how well you apply the lessons that have just been tackled in this chapter. Use the appropriate greeting/ term/ word for the situations given below.

1. Provide the appropriate greeting for the following:
   a) 8:00
   b) 16:00
   c) 19:00
   d) Bedtime
2. A vendor in a boutique has offered to sell you a trinket but you are not interested.
   a) *No*
   b) *Per favore*
   c) *Mi dispiace*
   d) *No, grazie*
3. You wish to call the attention of someone.
4. How do you respond when someone thanks you?
5. You've just ended a dinner party with friend. How do you say goodbye?
6. You'd like to ask a friend for a favor, how do you begin your sentence?
7. You accidentally bumped into a stranger. How do you make an apology?
8. You bumped into an acquaintance and they have asked you how you have been. How do you ask how he's doing?

9. You walk into a boutique and you would like to know if they shopkeeper speaks English. What do you ask him?

10. Someone has been explaining directions to you but you did not understand. How do you ask them politely to speak slowly and repeat the instructions?

Answer key:

1) & b. Buongiorno; c. Buonasera; d. Buonanotte
2) d. No, grazie
3) Scusi
4) prego
5) Ciao
6) Per favore
7) Mi dispiace
8) Molto bene, grazie... Come sta?
9) Buongiorno / Buonasera, parla Inglese?
10) Scusi / Prego? Parli più lentamente

CHAPTER 2:
INTRODUCTIONS AND PLEASANTRIES

In this chapter we will cover the following topics:
- Introducing yourself
- Asking about others and getting to know them
- Say no or to deny something

Articulation:
Below is a list of the common words and phrases we will be using in this chapter.

Come ['kome]	*How*
Si chiama [see kja'ma]	*You are called;* *He is called;* *She is called;* *It is called...*
Mi chiamo [mi kja'mo]	*I call myself;* *I am called*
Chi? [khi] / [qi]	*Who?*
È / è: [ē]	*You/ He/She/It* *(Pronoun)*
Chi è Lei? [khi ē 'lay] / [qi ē 'lay]	*Who are you?* *Who is she?*
Chi è lui? [khi ē 'lui] / [qi ē 'lui]	*Who is he?*
Che [khe] / [qe]	*Who/whom/which/that* *(Relative to something)*
(Io) sono ['sono]	*I am*

(Io) non sono [non 'sono]	*I am not*
Non è [non e]	*You are not* *He/She/It is not*
Questo è [kwesto e]	*This is*
Bambino/ Bambina [bam-bi-no] [bam-bi-na]	*A child (boy/girl)*
(Io) piacere [pee-a-chay-ray]	*I am pleased to meet you* *It is a pleasure to meet you*
Si accomodi / **s'accomodi** [see ak-omo'di] [s'ak-omo'di]	*Come in*
Soltanto [sol'tanto]	*Only*
Ma [ma]	*But*
Mia moglie [mia moll'e]	*My wife*
Nostra figlia [nos-tra fil-yah] [nos-tra filla']	*Our daughter*
Straniero/ Straniera [stran-ye-ro] [stran-ye-ra]	*A foreigner (man/ woman)* *Alien* *Stranger*

Reminders:
- The word **chi** is used when asking a question.
- **Che** is often included in the sentence and cannot be omitted similar to the English language.
- Shortening words or combining them together can convert the meaning into a phrase or sentence. Combining words are usually denoted by a apostrophe (').

Practice conversations and dialogues (Dialoghi)

<u>Scenario:</u> You are invited to a party. You introduce yourself and mingle amongst the other guests.

- Dialogue 1 – Introducing yourself
  Michel Morretti: *Ciao! Io sono Michel Morretti. Come si chiama?*
  You: *Ciao! Mi chiamo _your name_.*
  Michel Morretti: *Piacere signora __your name__!*
- Dialogue 2 – Looking for a specific person
  You: *Scusi, Lei è la signor Verdi?*
  Paolo Pucci: *No, non sono il signor Verdi.*
  You: *Come si chiama?*
  Paolo Pucci: *Mi chiamo Paolo Pucci.*

Quick tips on syntax and proper use of words:

- Nouns are gender based in Italian
  - Italian names for men usually end with an "o" (Mario) whereas women's names often end with an "a" (Francesca).
  - The same rule applies to other things in *Italiano.* Nouns are gender based. Some are feminine and some are masculine.
  - Like with women's names, feminine nouns often end with an "a".
  - Masculine nouns do not always end with an "o". Some end with an "e".
- Articles: *il, la, un, una, questo, questa*
  - Articles *il, la, un, una, questo* and *questa* are the equivalent of the words **he, she, it** and **the** in the English language.
  - **Il** – this article is often associated with masculine nouns. It is the equivalent of the article "the" in the English language.
    - *Il tenore* (The tenor)
    - *Il libro* (The book)
    - *Il cane* (The dog)

- La – is the counterpart of **il.** It is used together with feminine nouns. It is the equivalent of the article "the" in the English language.
  - *La banca* (The bank)
  - *La voce* (The voice)
  - *La mamma* (The mother)
- **Un / Una –** these articles are used preceding both masculine and feminine nouns. It is the equivalent of the article "a" in the English language.
  - *Una penna* (A pen)
  - *Un libro* (A book)
  - *Un treno* (A train)
- **Questo / Questa** - these articles are the counterparts of the article "this is" in the English language. They are also used preceding nouns that are either masculine or feminine, respectively.
  - *Questo il tenore*
  - *Questo un treno*
  - *Questa la banca*
  - *Questa una penna*
- Words that depict action – Verb
  Verbs, in Italian, function in the same manner as those in the English language. These are words that depict or express a particular action. Examples of common verbs used in Italian are: **parlo, sono** and **è.** When you wish to negate something, you simply add the word **non** (as shown in the examples above).
  Verbs are preceded by pronouns such as "*I, you, she, he and it*". These subject pronouns are not used in a similar manner when translating into Italian. The only exception to this rule is the use of **Lei.**
- Adjectives
  - In the Italian language, adjectives are categorized into either feminine or masculine.

- Note: Nationalities do not require a capitalized first letter as shown below:

Nationalities: (Nazionalità)

Lei è (Feminine)	australiana	Lui è (Masculine)	australiano	Australian
	austriaca		austriaco	Austrian
	tedesca		tedesco	German
	spagnola		spagnolo	Spanish
	svizzera		svizzero	Swiss
	britannica		britannico	British
	inglese		inglese	English
	americana		americano	American
	scozzese		scozzese	Scottish
	gallese		gallese	Welsh
	irlandese		irlandese	Irish
	portoghese		portoghese	Portuguese
	neozelandese		neozelandese	Newzealander
	canadese		canadese	Canadian
	francese		francese	French

Note that nationalies that end with **-ese** are the same for both feminine and masculine adjectives.

- Names and titles
  - Similar to adjectives, Italian names are often gender based – either feminine or masculine.

19

CHAPTER 3:
NUMBERS, COUNTING AND PLURAL NOUNS

In this chapter we will cover the following topics:
- Learning to count in Italian. (From 0-19; 20 and higher).
- The general rules of counting and exceptions to these rules.
- Common phrases used when talking about numbers and when counting
- Keywords and phrases pertaining to buying and inquiring
- Transforming phrases in the singular form to their plural form
- General rules on changing nouns from singular form to their plural counterpart.
- Simple conversation on how to order and purchase items from a clerk / vendor.

Counting in Italian:
Learning to count in a foreign language can feel complicated at first. The upside is that some (but not all) numbers are quite similar to their English counterparts. There are some slight differences but all it takes is a bit of memory work. It is essential to learn the basic numerals in Italian especially if you are planning to travel to Italy.

Numbers are a part of every day life. Money, time and dates are only a few of the things you will require a substantial knowledge about numbers. When we talk about finances, it's not only safe but also smart to be able to communicate well especially when you're in a foreign country. No one wants to be stuck in a foreign country without money or lost somewhere because you missed the last train since you didn't understand the time and date posted on the schedule board.

The rule when counting in Italian is that there is a unique term for the numbers 0 up to 16. Numbers from 17 and above add on to each other to define a particular numeral. Examples are shown below.

Zero / Nought	**0**	Zero
Uno	**1**	One
Due	**2**	Two
Tre	**3**	Three
Quattro	**4**	Four
Cinque	**5**	Five
Sei	**6**	Six
Sette	**7**	Seven
Otto	**8**	Eight
Nove	**9**	Nine
Dieci	**10**	Ten
Undici	**11**	Eleven
Dodici	**12**	Twelve
Tredici	**13**	Thirteen
Quattordici	**14**	Fourteen
Quindici	**15**	Fifteen
Sedici	**16**	Sixteen
Dicissette	**17**	Seventeen
Diciotto	**18**	Eighteen
Diciannove	**19**	Nineteen

For numbers in the twenties, thirties, forties and higher, you just need to add the value to the tenths (see the example below for clarification).

Exception: when adding the numerals 1 and 8, you must drop the last letter (which is "i") and combine the two words.

Also, when adding the numeral three or *tre* to the tenths, the last "e".

As for larger numbers, the same rules apply to those in the tenths.

Venti	**20**	Twenty
Ventuno	**21**	Twenty one
Ventidue	**22**	Twenty two
Trenta	**30**	Thirty
Trentuno	**31**	Thirty one
Trentadue	**32**	Thirty two
Quaranta	**40**	Forty
Quarantuno	**41**	Forty one
Quarantadue	**42**	Forty two
Cinquanta	**50**	Fifty
Sessanta	**60**	Sixty
Settanta	**70**	Seventy
Ottanta	**80**	Eighty
Novanta	**90**	Ninety
Cento	**100**	One hundred
Centuno	**101**	One hundred one
Centodue	**102**	One hundred two
Centocinquanta	**150**	One hundred fifty
Mille	**1,000**	One thousand
Duemila	**2,000**	Two thousand

Practice tips:
- Now that we've covered counting numerals, you can practice your skills by taking a phonebook and practice reading numbers in Italian. Read it aloud so that you're able to practice articulation as well.
- Writing down numbers can also help you retain information.
- Pace yourself. Go slow at first and eventually pick up speed to improve on your fluency and memory.

Grammar:

In English, when using plural nouns, we usually add an **–s** to the end of the noun. In Italian, a noun is transformed into its plural form by changing the last vowel of the noun. The rules are as follows:

- For nouns that end with an **–o** or **–e**, these are generally changed to an **–i:**
    - *Libro : Libri [Book : Books]*
    - *Automobile : Automobili [Car : Cars]*
    - ***Exception:** Cani : Cani [Dog : Dogs]*
- For nouns that end with an **–a**, these are generally changed to an **–e:**
    - *Ragazza : Ragazze [Girl : Girls]*
    - *Donna : Donne [Woman : Women]*
    - *Domanda : Domande [Question : Questions]*
- For articles preceding nouns (**il** & **la**), these articles transform to complement plural nouns as well. **Il** is transformed into **i** whereas, **la** is changed to **le:**
    - *il treno : i treni [the train : the trains]*
    - *la penna : le penne [the pen : the pens]*
- For articles preceding nouns (**questo** & **questa**), these articles transform to complement plural nouns as well. **Questo** is transformed into **questi** whereas, **questa** is changed to **queste:**
    - *Questo libro : questi libri [this book : these books]*
    - *Questa donna : queste donne [this woman : these women]*

Note: Nouns ending in an accented vowel do not change their form and remain as is (e.g *cani).*

Articulation:

Below are some common words and phrases we will be using in this chapter.

Desidera [deside'ra]	*Can I help you?*
Mi dia [mi dee-ya]	*I will have*
Vorrei... [vo-rey]	*I would like*
Un caffè/ un capuccino [un ka-fe] [un ka-pu-chi-no]	*One coffee [espresso]* *One capuccino*
Un chilo di [un ki-lo di]	*A kilo of...*
Mezzo chilo di [med-zo ki-lo di]	*Half a kilo of...*
Quant'è? ['kwante]	*How much is it?*
Quanto costa? [kwanto kos-ta']	*How much does it cost?*
Quanto costano? [kwanto kos-ta-no']	*How much do they cost?*
È troppo [ē trop'-po] **È caro** [ē 'karo]	*It is much expensive* *It is too expensive*
È a buon mercato [ē a bwon mer'kato] **Costa poco** ['kosta 'poko]	*It is cheap* *It is inexpensive*
Deve pagare alla cassa ['de-ve pa'gare 'alla 'kas-a]	*You should pay at the cashier*
Deve fare lo scontrino ['de-ve 'fare lo skon'trino]	*You should take the receipt*

Practice conversations and dialogues (Dialoghi)

- Dialogue 1 – You visit an Italian bar. It says that you need to pay as you order.
  Waitress / Barista: *Buongiorno, signore!*
  You: *Buongiorno. Un caffè un panino.*

Waitress / Barista: *Deve fare lo scontrino*
You: *(You walk towards the cashiers desk...) Un caffè un panino, per favore.*
Cashier / Cassiera: *Come vuole il panino: con prosciutto, formaggio, salame, omelette...?*
You: *Prosciutto cotto o crudo?*
Cashier / Cassiera: *Come preferisce.*
You: *Allora con prosciutto crudo.*
Cashier / Cassiera: *Va bene. Un caffe e un panino con prosciutto crudo. Due e trentotto.*
You: *Due e trentotto... (You hand your payment to the cashier). Grazie.*
Cashier / Cassiera: *Prego.*

- Dialogue 2 – You've been craving for fruits all day. You visit the local country market to ask how much it costs to purchase a kilo of fruits and vegetables so that you can take home some produce.
Fruit vendor / Fruttivendola: *Desidera?*
You: *Quanto costano le mele?*
Fruit vendor / Fruttivendola: *Queste mele costano uno e ventinove; quelle due e sette.*
You: *Vorrei un chilo di queste. Le albicocche quanto costano?*
Fruit vendor / Fruttivendola: *Due e sette al chilo.*
You: *Sono troppo care. Mi dia un chilo di ciliege.*
Fruit vendor / Fruttivendola: *Ecco. Desidera altro, signora?*
You: Sì. *Mezzo chilo di pomodori, non troppo maturi.*
Fruit vendor / Fruttivendola: *Questi vanno bene?*
You: Sì, grazie. È tutto. Quant'è in tutto?
Fruit vendor / Fruttivendola: *Allora... le mele due e sette, le ciliege uno e novantasei, I pomodori cinquantadue centesimi... Quattro e cinquantacinque in tutto.*
You: *Ecco cinque euro...*
Fruit vendor / Fruttivendola: *Grazie. Ecco quarantacinque centesimi di resto.*

CHAPTER 4:
DATE AND TIME

In this chapter we will cover the following topics:
- How to tell the time and use it in a conversation.
- How to ask someone what time it is.
- Engage someone else in a conversation about an upcoming event or current events.
- Learn the days of the week and the months of the year

Before you continue on with this chapter, remember that asking the time and inquiring about something related to dates and time are inevitable. This is the reason why this chapter covers numerous keywords and phrases that you can put to good use especially when travelling abroad. That way, you won't feel bombarded with foreign terminologies when the opportunity presents itself.

As you learn to tell time and say the dates, practice it more often – on a daily or hourly basis. Think of appointments and other things you have schedule on your planner and try to translate these into Italian as well.

Recap activity:
Before we proceed with the lesson, here's a short recap of the previous chapter. Note that this will be very useful since numerals are also covered in this section. Recite the numerals below out loud in *Italiano*.

67	5	15	28	12	48	31	6	7	17

Articulation:
Below is a list of the common words and phrases we will be covering in this chapter.

Che ore sono? / che ora è? [ke ore 'sono] / [ke ora ē]	*What is the time? /* *What time is it?*
Sono le __ e __ ['sono le] __ [ē] __ **Sono le <u>due</u> e <u>dieci</u>?** ['sono le 'due ē 'dye-chee]	*It is __ past __ /* *It is <u>ten</u> past <u>two</u>.*
Quando arriva l'aero? ['kwando ar-riva l'ay-ro]	*When will the plane arrive?*
A che ora? [a kē ora']	*What time...*
Apre la banca? ['a-pre la ban-ka]	*Will the bank open? /* *Does the bank open?*
Comincia il film? [komin'chare il film] **Inizia il film?** [ini'tsya il film]	*Does the movie/ film start?*
Finisce lo spettacolo? [fini-che lo spet-ta-kolo]	*Will the show end? /* *Does the show end?*
Apron gli uffici? [apron lyi ufichi]	*Will the offices open? /* *Do the offices open?*
Chiudono i museo? [kyu-dono y mu'zeo]	*Will the museum close? /* *Does the museum close?*
Finiscono di lavorare? [finiskono di lavorare]	*Will they finish work? /* *Do they finish work?*
È la prima colazione...? [è la prima' kola'tsone]	*Is breakfast...?*
È la seconda colazione...? [è la sekonda kola'tsone] **il pranzo...?** [il 'prandzo]	*Is lunch...?*
La cena? [la 'tsena]	*Is dinner...?*
Quanto dura? [kwanto dura]	*How long does it last? /* *Does it last long?*
Dalle __ alle __	*From __ to __ /*

[dal-le __ al-le __] **Dalle sette alle dieci** [dal-le set-te al-le 'dyet-chee]	*From 7 to 10*
Dura due ore? [dura due ore]	*It takes two hours*
Tardi [tar-di] **Presto** [pres-'to]	*Late/* *Early*
Ieri [ye-ri]	*Yesterday*
L'altro ieri [l'atro ye-ri]	*The day before yesterday*
Questa mattina [kwesta mat-tina] **stamattina** [sta-mat-tina]	*This morning*
Questa sera [kwesta se-ra] **stasera** [stasera]	*This evening*
Oggi [od-ji]	*Today*
Che giorno è oggi? [ke djor-no e od-ji]	*Today is? /* *What is the day today?*
Domani ['domani]	*Tomorrow*
Dopodomani ['dop-po-domani]	*The day after tomorrow*
Fra una settimana [fra u-na set-ti'mana]	*In a week or so... /* *In a week's time...*
È chiusa [e kyu-sa]	*Its closed*
All'ora di pranzo [al-yora di 'prandzo]	*During lunch / At lunch*

Riaprono [ri-yah-pro-no]	*Re-open / Open again*
Dappertutto [dap-er'tutt-o]	*Everywhere / In all places*
Alcune città [al-kune tsi-ta']	*In some cities / In some towns*
Mezz'ora piu tardi [med'dzora pyu tar-di]	*After half an hour / Half an hour later*
Ci vediamo [tsi ved'iamo]	*Until then / See you soon / We'll see each other (soon)...*
È troppo lontano [e trop-po lontano]	*It's very far*

Parts of the day: (Parti del giorno)

La mattina	*Morning*
	In the morning
Questa mattina	*This morning*
Il pomeriggio	*Afternoon*
	In the afternoon
Questo pomeriggio	*This afternoon*
La sera	*Evening*
	In the evening
Questa sera	*This evening*
La note	*Night*
	At night
Questa note	*Tonight*
La note scorsa	*Last night*
L'alba	*Dawn*
Il tramonto	*Sunset*

The days of the week: (*I giorno della settimana*)

lunedì	*Monday*
martedì	*Tuesday*
mercoledì	*Wednesday*
giovedì	*Thursday*
venerdì	*Friday*

sabato	*Saturday*
domenica	*Sunday*
il fine settimana l'weekend	*The weekend*
lunedì prossimo lunedì scorso	*Next Monday* *Last Monday*

The months of the year: (I mesi dell'anno)

gennaio	*January*
febbraio	*February*
marzo	*March*
aprile	*April*
maggio	*May*
giugno	*June*
luglio	*July*
agosto	*August*
settembre	*September*
ottobre	*October*
novembre	*November*
dicembre	*December*
il mese il gennaio prossimo il agosto scorso	*Next month* *Next February* *Last August*

The four seasons: (Le quattro stagioni)

primavera	*Spring*
estate	*Summer*
autunno	*Autumn*
inverno	*Winter*
L'estate prossima L'autunno scorsa	*Next summer* *Last summer*

Note:

In Italian, the first letter of the days of the week, months of the year and seasons is not capitalized unlike those in the English language.

Practice conversations and dialogues (Dialoghi)

- Dialogo 1

  You approach the hotel staff to ask for the time since you need to take medications. Unfortunately you are unsure if you will be too early or late to the pharmacy.

  You: *Scusi, che ore sono?*

  Hotel staff: *Sono le tre e dieci*

  You: *Devo comprare una medicina ma la farmaia è chiusa.*

  Hotel staff: *È troppo presto. La farmacia apre alle tre e mezzo. Deve ritornare piuú tardi.*

- Dialogo 2

  The next day, you plan to visit several shops around the city and you'd like to inquire at the tourist office to check what time they open during the afternoon.

  You: *Buongiorno. Quando aprono i negozi?*

  Tourist office personnel: *La mattina?*

  You: *Sì.*

  Tourist office personnel: *La mattina aprono alle otto e mezzo.*

  You: *Chiudono all'ora di pranzo?*

  Tourist office personnel: Sì, alle dodici e mezzo.

  [You inquire about another shop...]

  You: *E il pomeriggio?*

  Tourist office personnel: *Il pomeriggio riaprono alle tre e mezzo e chiudono alle sette e mezzo.*

  You: *Grazie. Buongiorno.*

  Tourist office personnel: *Buongiorno.*

- Dialogo 3

  Marinella and Francesca are best friends. They are planning to watch a movie at the cinema and talk about where they are going to meet [At the Piazza Garibaldi].

  Marinella: *A che ora comincia il film?*

  Francesca: *Alle nove.*

  Marinella: *Allora ci vediamo alle nove meno un quarto?*

Francesca: *Va bene. Dove?*

Marinella: *Al bar Smeraldo. Va bene?*

Francesca: *No, è troppo lontano. Puoi venire in piazza Garibaldi.*

Marinella: *Va bene, ci vediamo in piazza Garibaldi. Ciao.*

Francesca: *Ciao.*

- Dialogo 4

  While riding the bus, you overhear a conversation between a little boy and his chaperon. The chaperon is asking the boy if he goes to Saturday school and if he has class in the afternoon.

  Chaperon: *Vai a scuola tutti i giorni?*

  Bambino: *Sì, tutti i giorni, eccetto la domenica.*

  Chaperon: *Allora vai a scuola anche il sabato!*

  Bambino: *Sì, anche il sabato: da ottobre a giugno.*

  Chaperon: *A che ora cominciano le lezioni?*

  Bambino: *Cominciano alle otto e mezzo e finiscono a mezzogiorno e mezzo.*

  Chaperon: *E il pomeriggio?*

  Bambino: *Il pomeriggio sto a casa a fare i compiti.*

Quick tips on syntax and proper use of words:

- When telling time...
  - There are two basic ways on how you can ask someone the time. You can either use **che ore sono?** Or **che ora è?** Either one is acceptable and formal. The answer to your query would begin with the phrase **sono le...** [Time].
  - The article **è** always precedes any particular word pertaining to a time of day such as those cited below:
    - *Midday:* **è mezzogirono**
    - *Midnight:* è **mezzanotte**
  - When giving the specific time of day, you must first cite the hour then followed by the

minutes. The word **minuti** is not always required when giving the time.

- o Formal announcements in *Italiano* are given using the 24-hour clock format.
- o Another way of giving time is to deduct the few minutes left before then succeeding hour, such as the case below. **Meno** literally translates to "minus".
    - *Twenty minutes to nine:* **Sono le nove meno venti**
    - *A quarter past nine:* ***Sono le nove meno un quarto.***
- On the days of the week...
    - o The days of the week are gender based meaning they are either feminine or masculine. All days of the week are considered masculine except for Sunday (*domenica*).
        - **il lunedi:** *Monday*
        - **la domenica:** *Sunday*
- On using 'yesterday' and 'tomorrow'
    - o The words **ieri, oggi, domain and dopodomani** do not change.
    - o The first three can be combined together with **pomeriggio, mattina** and **serra.**
    - o **Oggi** can only be put together with **pomeriggio.**
        - **Ieri sera:** *yesterday evening*
        - **Domani mattina:** *tomorrow morning*
        - **Oggi pomeriggio:** *this afternoon*

CHAPTER 5:
GOING THE DISTANCE: MASTERING THE LANGUAGE BY HEART

Congratulations! You've reached the last chapter of this book. Italian is a beautiful language that is learnt not only through memory but also with the heart. This book is only but the beginning to a wonderful adventure that you are about to embark on.

Many people dream of learning a new language and being able to speak it fluently. That is truly one big achievement. However, we don't all learn at the same pace. It takes different approaches for different people to master a new language. We may remember a phrase here and there but unfortunately, with lack of practice [and exposure] the skills we learn are soon forgotten.

It is a sad waste of effort on the learner's part. As a beginner, you should know that you must practice and immerse yourself in the culture so that you do not forget.

If you are truly determined to know the language by heart, here are some tips on how you can improve your *l'italiano*.
1. ***Listen, listen and then listen some more***.
   Always keep your ears open. It is not enough to just be able to speak the language. Communication requires understanding and the skill of listening. Italians are very expressive when they talk so observe and fill your ears. The Internet is a wonderful place to begin acquiring resources especially if you do not know anyone who is fluent in the language. Take the time to listen to recording and podcasts to help you catch on with the vernacular.

2. *Always carry a part of Italy with you.*

Going for a trip to Italy can be costly. Right now might not seem like such a good idea to go on a luxurious trip. But this does not mean that you cannot bring Italy with you. Do things that are Italian in nature – listen to Italian music, eat some authentic Italian pasta, and drink an espresso and the like... In other words, immerse yourself in the culture.

Remember, there is a saying: *"You can take the girl out of Italy, but you can't take Italy out of the girl!"*

3. *Practice at least one Italian word a day.*

Practice makes perfect. Train yourself to remember Italian terms for everyday objects. Seeing a mundane object and associating an Italian term with it helps to sharpen the memory. Soon you'll be able to use Italian terms on a daily basis. If you're having a hard time at first, put up labels or cue cards on objects to help you remember. Don't remove the labels until you're certain that you've remembered them all by heart. One Italian word a day keeps the memory gaps away!

4. *Expand your vocabulary.*

Be hungry for knowledge. Go out and find yourself a good English-Italian dictionary. Once you have one, find an article written in Italian and learn to translate this written work into English. This serves as a good practice in terms of words and conjugating sentences. It's a fun and challenging way to learn different words and how to properly use them.

Purchase or borrow books and magazines that are written in Italian. As a beginner, try to find books that are written in simplified forms of Italian. This is especially important if you're planning on reading Italian short stories and novels. Another option is to look for dual language books, which have an English translation incorporated in the book as well. Newspapers are also a good place to start looking for articles. Not only are you learning Italian but also keeping up with the current events.

You can expand to random words in a book or dictionary. Pick a random word for the day and remember how it is spoken as well as how it is written. Pick one word per day and by the end of the week, you'll have seven words. Recall each one and try to use it in a sentence.

5. *Fill your ears with music.*

If you ever get tired of reading or translating articles, you can always opt for something a little more entertaining. Listen to Italian music and try to dissect the words. Ask yourself, what words are you able to isolate from the lyrics of the song? Does it make any sense to you?

If you're having a difficult time following the lyrics of a song, put your Internet skills to good use and download the lyrics. Singing along to a tune may also help you with your articulation. What better way to learn Italian words than with a song!

6. *Explore and get to know Italian movies.*

Enjoy a movie or two in Italian. Yes, it can be difficult to read the subtitles but that's not the point. Study the manner on how the actors express themselves. Italians, as mentioned earlier, are very expressive when they talk. This provides an insight on how to properly articulate and express oneself. It also helps you to practice your listening and comprehension skills at the same time.

Start with a few classics and work your way up to newer and recent flicks. If you can, jot down some expressions and phrases – especially the ones you don't understand. That way, after the movie you can look it up in your dictionary.

7. *Learn other forms of entertainment.*

Learning to play a variety of Italian games can also be quite helpful when you are trying to learn the language. Not only does it challenge your vocabulary, it also hones your skills of comprehension. Crossword puzzles are a good place to start as well as other simple word games. You could even turn the learning experience into a group activity.

8. ***Meet Italian people or native speakers of the language.***

If you look hard enough, chances are you'll be able to find someone who is fluent in the language. Go to an Italian restaurant, a cafè or cultural affairs. There are numerous ways on how you can meet someone whose native tongue is *Italiano*. Making friends with someone who knows the language well can help you hone and develop your skills of communication.

9. ***Do not be afraid to make mistakes. Do not be afraid to engage someone in conversation.***

Remember, you are in the process of learning. And as you do, there will be times that you will make mistakes. Do not be ashamed if you do not pronounce words properly the first few times. This is expected. The important thing is that you do not give up. If you happen to be at a loss for words, use your hands and express yourself in this manner. If anything, gestures are truly at the heart of communicating in Italian. *Molto Italiano!*

Keep a notebook and note down the words that you commonly forget or mispronounce. Take the time to say these out loud each day - about 4-5 times per word/ phrase or sentence.

10. ***Have the passion for the language. Love what you are doing.***

No matter how complicated the language may be if you have the passion to learn it, you will succeed. You may not be a native speaker but that does not mean you won't get good at it. Do not feel discourage if at the end of this book you still feel like there is a lot to learn. The reality is that there is a lot more to learn

37

but if you took the contents of this book seriously, you'll bring with you a good foundation of the Italian language from which you can build on. The basics are the essential things that you must learn before you head on to more complex phrases, expressions and the like.

What you must understand is that these things take time. Be patient with yourself. Take it one step at a time. This book is the start of a long and exciting learning process. Do not rush yourself to the finish line other wise you'll end up back right where you started.

No matter what motivates you to push further to learn the language, take the opportunity and challenge yourself. Learning a second language develops not only, your personality but also, your communication, analytic and interpretative skills as well. It opens doors for you. It expands your vocabulary and provides you with bigger opportunities in the future.

BONUS CHAPTER:
10 USEFUL DIALOGUES YOU CAN PRACTICE IN ITALY

Dialogue1: *L'arrivo all'aeroporto di Milano: al bar/ Arriving to the Milan's airport: at the bar*

Italian
Waiter *Buongiorno, mi dica.*
Tom *Buongiorno. Vorrei un caffè, un cappuccino e un'acqua minerale.*
Waiter *Si. Al banco o al tavolo?*
Tom *Al banco.*
Waiter *Mi dispiace, deve fare lo scontrino alla cassa. Prego, da*
questa parte.
Tom *Un caffè, un cappuccino e un'acqua minerale. Quant'è?*
Waiter: *Sono €2 e 90 centesimi. Ecco il resto e lo scontrino.*

At the bar:
Tom*Un caffe,un cappuccino bollente e un'acqua minerale naturale.*
Waitress *Ecco il caffè, il cappuccino e la minerale.*
Tom *Grazie.*

English
Waiter *Good morning, how may I help?*
Tom *Good morning. I would like a coffee, a cappuccino and a mineral water.*
Waiter *Yes, at the bar or sitting down?*
Tom At the bar.
Waiter *I am sorry, you must get a till receipt. Please, this way.*
Tom *A coffee, a cappuccino and a mineral water. How much is it?*

Waiter *It's €2 and 90 cents. Here is the change and the receipt.*

At the bar:
Tom *A coffee, a boiling hot cappuccino and a still mineral water.*
Waitress *Here's the coffee, the cappuccino and the mineral water.*
Tom *Thanks.*

Dialogue 2: L'arrivo alla stazione centrale di Milano: Prendere il taxi/ arriving at the Milan's Central Station: taking the taxi

Italian
Taxi driver *Buongiorno.*
Kim *Buongiorno. Dobbiamo andare all'albergo Lancaster.*
Taxi driver *In quale via?*
Kim *In via Abbondio Sangiorgio.*
Taxi driver *A quale numero?*
Kim *Al numero 16, credo.*
Taxi driver *Va bene, al numero 16 di via Abbondio Sangiorgio.*
Taxi driver *Ecco l'albergo Abbondio Sangiorgio. Sono € 20.*
Kim *Bene, grazie. Ecco a lei.*
Taxi driver *Grazie, arrivederci.*

English
Taxi driver *Good morning.*
Kim *Good morning. We need to go to the Hotel Regina Margherita.*
Taxi driver *In which street?*
Kim *In Abbondio Sangiorgio street.*
Taxi driver *Which number is the hotel?*
Kim *At number 16, I think.*
Taxi driver *OK, to number 16, in Abbondio Sangiorgio street.*
Taxi driver *Here is the Hotel Lancaster. It's €20.*

Kim *Good, thank you. Here you are.*
Taxi driver *Thank you. Goodbye.*

Dialogue 3: All'albergo/at the hotel

Italian
Signora Benedetti *Buongiorno!*
Kim *Buongiorno, signora. Vorremmo una camera singola per questa sera e domani sera.*
Signora Benedetti *Ho una camera singola Iibera per questa sera.*
Kim *Bene. Quanto costa?*
Signora Benedetti *Sono €80 per notte.*
Kim *La colazione è compresa?*
Signora Benedetti *La prima colazione è compresa. Avete il Passaporto (o carta d'identità)?*
Kim *ecco i passaporti.*
Signora Benedetti *Benissimo, ecco le chiavi.*
Kim *Grazie. A stasera.*
Signora Benedetti *Arrivederci e grazie.*

English
Signora Benedetti *Good morning!*
Kim *Good morning, Madam. I would like a single room for tonight and tomorrow night.*
Signora Benedetti *Yes. I have a vacant single room from tonight.*
Kim *Fine. How much is it?*
Signora Benedetti *It's € 80 per night.*
Kim *Is breakfast included?*
Signora Benedetti *Yes, breakfast is included. Have you got your
passport?*
Kim *Yes, here are the passports.*
Signora Benedetti *Fine, here are the keys.*
Kim *Thanks. See you tonight.*

41

Signora Benedetti *Thank you and goodbye.*

Dialogue 4: Al ristorante/ at the restaurant

This chapter is divided in two parts:
1)Ordinare un tavolo/ Booking a table
2)Mangiare(avere un pasto) / Having a meal

Part 1) Ordinare un tavolo/ Booking a table
Italian
Kim *Buonasera, vorrei prenotare un tavolo per due.*
Waitress *Per quando?*
Kim *Per domani.*
Waitress *Per mezzogiorno o per la sera?*
Kim *La sera va benissimo.*
Waitress *A che ora?*
Kim *Per le otto, otto e mezza.*
Waitress *Va bene per le otto e mezza?*
Kim *Grazie. Accettate carte di credito?*
Waitress *Si certamente*
Kim *Benissimo. A domani.*
Waitress *Arrivederci e grazie.*

English
Kim *Good evening, I would like to book a table for two.*
Waitress *When for?*
Kim *For tomorrow.*
Waitress *Lunchtime or evening?*
Kim *The evening is fine.*
Waitress *At what time?*
Kim *For 8 or for 8.30.*
Waitress *Is 8.30 OK?*
Kim *Thank you. Do you take credit cards?*
Waitress *Yes, except ... this card.*
Kim *Fine, see you tomorrow.*
Waitress *Thank you and goodbye.*

Part 2: Having a meal
Italian
Waitress *Buonasera. Desidera?*
Tom *Buonasera. Ho un tavolo per due per le otto e mezza.*
Waitress *Ah, si, lei è il signor Miller?*
Tom *Si.*
Waitress *Prego, da questa parte.*
Tom *Vorrei del vino bianco della casa e un'acqua minerale.*
Waitress *Ecco il vino e la minerale.*
Tom *Grazie, cosa c'e nel menu del giorno?*
Waitress *Di primi, tortelli di zucca, penne o bigoli al ragu*
Tom *Due tortelli di zucca.*
At the end of the meal:
Tom *Vorrei due caffe e il conto.*
Waitress *Ecco. Sono € 24.*
Tom *Accettate la Visa?*
Waitress *Si, non c'e problema.*

English
Waitress *Good evening. How can I help?*
Tom *Good evening. I have a table for two for half past eight.*
Waitress *Ah, yes, is he mr Miller?.*
Tom *Yes.*
Waitress *Please, this way.*
Tom *I would like some house white wine and a mineral water.*
Waitress *Here's the wine and the mineral water.*
Tom *Thank you, what are the specials of the day?*
Waitress *As a first course, pumpkin tortelli, penne or bigoli with*
ragu.
Tom *Two pumpkin tortelli.*
At the end of the meal:
Tom *I would like two coffees and the bill.*
Waitress *Here you are. It's €24.*
Tom *Do you accept Visa?*
Waitress *Yes, no problem.*

Dialogue 5: Alla stazione di polizia /Going to the police station

Italian
Receptionist *Buongiorno. Mi dica.*
Tom *Buongiorno. Ho un problema. Penso di avere perso il passaporto e il problema è che ritorno in Inghilterra tra due giorni.*
Receptionist *Faccia Ia dichiarazione di smarrimento del documento.*
Tom *Che cosa è?*
Receptionist *Compili con i suoi dati personali e il numero del passaporto.*
Tom *Che cosa mi consiglia di fare?*
Receptionist *Contatti il Consolato britannica per il passaporto sostitutivo. Ecco il numero di telefono.*
Tom *Arrivederci e grazie.*
Receptionist *Grazie a lei.*

English
Receptionist *Good morning. How can I help?*
Tom *Good morning. I have a problem. I think I have lost my passport and the problem is that I am returning to England in two days time.*
Receptionist *Complete (do) a document loss report.*
Tom *What is that?*
Receptionist *Fill it in (complete) with your personal details and the Passport number.*
Tom *What do you suggest I do?*
Receptionist *Contact the British Consulate for a replacement passport. Here is the telephone number.*
Tom *Thank you and goodbye.*
Receptionist *Thank you.*

Dialogue 6: Fare shopping / Going shopping

Italian

Assistant *Buongiorno. Desidera?*

Kim *Buongiorno. Posso dare un'occhiata alla borsa rossa in vetrina?*

Assistant *Si. Ecco a lei. Le piace?*

Kim *Si, ma è troppo grande.*

Assistant *Ho questo modello nuovo; e molto pratico da portare.*

Kim *La borsa è bella, ma non mi piace il colore.*

Assistant *Mi dispiace, ma questa modello è disponibile solo marrone. E' molto di moda.*

Kim *Va bene. Quanta costa?*

Assistant *Costa solo € 49.*

Kim *Non è cara. Va benissimo, la compro. Ecco la carta di credito.*

English

Assistant *Good morning. Can I help you?*

Kim *Good morning. Can I have a look at the red handbag in the shop window?*

Assistant *Yes. Here you are. Do you like it?*

Kim *Yes, but it is too big.*

Assistant *I have got this new design; it is very practical to wear.*

Kim *The bag is nice, but I don't like the colour.*

Assistant *I am sorry, but this design is only available in brown. It is*
very much in fashion.

Kim *OK. How much does it cost?*

Assistant *It costs only € 49.*

Kim *It's not expensive. OK, I'll buy it. Here is the credit card.*

Dialogue 7: Prendere il bus/ Getting a bus

Italian
Tom *Buonasera. Vorrei 2(due) biglietti per il tram.*
Employee *Ecco a lei, sono €3.*
Tom *Grazie. Vorrei un'informazione. Quale tram arriva in Piazza Castello?*
Employee *Il numero 27.*
Tom *A che ora parte?*
Employee *Il numero 27 parte ogni sei minuti.*
Tom *Da dove parte?*
Employee *La fermata è di fronte alla fermata Cairoli.*
Tom *Grazie.*

English
Tom *Good evening. I would like 2 tram tickets.*
Employee *Here you are, it's €3.*
Tom *Thank you. I would like some information. Which tram arrives in Piazza Castello?*
Employee *The number 27.*
Tom *At what time does it leave?*
Employee *The number 27 leaves every six minutes.*
Tom *Where does it leave from?*
Employee *The tram stop is in front of the Cairoli metro stop .*
Tom *Thank you.*

Dialogue 8: Prendere il treno / Getting a train

Italian
Kim *Buongiorno. Vorrei due biglietti per Verona Porta Nuova.*
Employee *Di sola andata?*
Kim *Si, di sola andata?.*
Employee *A che ora deve arrivare a Verona?*
Kim *Devo essere a Verona per le due del pomeriggio.*
Employee *C'e un treno Intercity Freccia Bianca alle 12:25; arriva a Verona alle 13:50.*

Kim *Sì, vu bene.*
Employee *In tutto sono € 43.*
Kim *Ecco a lei. Da dove parte il treno?*
Employee *Dal binario 14.*
Kim *Grazie, arrivederci.*

English
Kim *Good morning. I would like two tickets to Verona.*
Employee *Return?*
Kim *No, single.*
Employee *At what time do you need to arrive in Verona?*
Kim *I need to be in Verona by 14:00 o'clock.*
Employee *There is an Intercity-Freccia Bianca train at 12.25; it arrives in Verona at 13.50.*
Kim *Yes, fine.*
Employee *Altogether that's €43.*
Kim *Here you are. From where does the train leave?*
Employee *From platform 14.*
Kim *Thank you. Goodbye.*

Dialogue 9: Andando al Duomo/ Going to the Duomo

Italian
Tom *Buongiorno. Vorrei delle informazioni sul Duomo
. Ha un depliant?*
Assistant *Penso di si, controllo subito. Ecco a lei! Che informazioni vuole?*
Tom *Quale e' l'orario di apertura?*
Assistant *Il museo fa orario continuato, dalle 7,00 fino alle 19,00.*
Tom *Tutti i giorni?*
Assistant *Si, tutti i giorni.*
Tom *Bene. E quanto costa l'ingresso?*
Assistant *Il biglietto intero, per la salita con l'ascensore, costa €12, quello ridotto €6. Per la salita a piedi invece, l'intero costa €7, e il ridotto costa €3,50.*

Tom *Benissimo, grazie. Ci sono visite guidate?*
Assistant *Si, deve prenotare.*
Tom *Quanta costa la visita guidata?*
Assistant *La visita e compresa nel biglietto.*
Tom *Grazie delle informazioni, arrivederci.*

English
Tom *Good morning. I would like some information about the Duomo, have you got a*
leaflet?
Assistant *I think so, I will check immediately. Here you are! What information do you want?*
Tom *What is the opening time?*
Assistant *The Duomo has continuous opening hours, from 7,00*
a.m. to 19,00 p.m.
Tom *Every day?*
Assistant *Every day.*
Tom *Good. And how much is the entrance ticket?*
Assistant *By lift: Full price €12.00; Reductions €6.00. On foot instead: Full price €7.00; Reductions €3.50*
Tom *Very well. Thank you. Are there guided tours?*
Assistant *Yes, you need to book.*
Tom *How much does a guided tour cost?*
Assistant *The tour is included in the admission price.*
Tim *Thank you for the information. Goodbye.*

Dialogue 10: Fare amicizia / Making friends

Italian
Signor DeNicola *Buongiorno. Anche a voi piace il caffe italiano!*
Kim *Si, molto.*
Signor DeNicola *E' la prima volta che visitate Verona?*
Kim *Si è la prima volta. Ora siamo qualche giorno a Milano ed bella, ma anche Verona*

molto bella. E voi siete qui in vacanza o per lavoro?
Signor DeNicola In vacanza e per motivi di famiglia. Siamo qui per il
matrimonio di mia sorella.
Kim Che bello! Quand'e il matrimonio?
Signor DeNicola E' oggi pomeriggio.
Kim Di dove siete?
Signor DeNicola Io sono di Torino e lei e polacca. E voi?
Kim Io sono di Londra e mio marito invece e' di New York.
Signor DeNicola Davvero? Io mi chiamo Carlo e lei e Natasha. Piacere!
Kim Io sono Kim e questo al mio fianco è Tim . Piacere!
Signor DeNicola Piacere! Piacere!

English
Signor DeNicola Good morning. You like Italian coffee too!
Kim Yes, very much.
Signor DeNicola Is this the first time you have visited Verona?
Kim Yes this is the first time. We are in Milan at the moment and I think that is a beautiful city, but also
Verona is so beautiful. And are you here on holiday
or business?
Signor DeNicola On holiday and for family reasons. We are here for
my sister's wedding.
Kim How nice! When is the wedding?
Signor DeNicola It's this afternoon.
Kim Where are you from?
Signor DeNicola I am from Turin and she is Polish. And you?
Jim I am from London , instead my husband is from New York.
Signor DeNicola Really? My name is Carlo and she is Natasha. Nice
to meet you!
Kim I am Kim and this is by my side is Tim. Nice to meet you!
Signor DeNicola Nice to meet you! Nice to meet you!

CONCLUSION

Thank you again for downloading this book!

I hope this book was able to help you to learn the basics of the Italian language. You have all the tools at your disposal; you just need to apply what you have read in the pages of this book.

The next step is to challenge yourself and be able to speak and communicate in Italian fluently. Italian is a beautiful language and you should give yourself a pat on the back for finishing this book but do not stop here. Expand your knowledge and challenge yourself through regular practice by utilizing different channels.

Finally, if you enjoyed this book, then I'd like to ask you for a favor, would you be kind enough to leave a review for this book on Amazon? It'd be greatly appreciated!

Please leave a review for this book on Amazon!
http://www.amazon.com/dp/B00Q5B49XM

Thank you and good luck!
Manuel De Cortes

CHECK OUT MY OTHER BOOKS

Below you'll find some of my other popular books that are popular on Amazon and Kindle as well. Simply click on the links below to check them out. Alternatively, you can visit my author page on Amazon to see other work done by me.

1) *Italian For Beginners: A practical guide to learn the basics of Italian in 10 days*
   http://www.amazon.com/dp/B00Q5B49XM
2) *Spanish For Beginners: A practical guide to learn the basics of Spanish in 10 days*
   http://www.amazon.com/dp/B00PLNCSAQ
3) *Italy Travel Guide: Top 40 Place You Can't Miss!*
   http://www.amazon.com/dp/B00M7V7PNA

34339359R00032

Made in the USA
Middletown, DE
17 August 2016